Serving Your Country

U.S. Army Special Operations

by Michael Green

Consultant:
Col. R. A. Jones, retired
U.S. Army SOF

CAPSTONE BOOKS
an imprint of Capstone Press
Mankato, Minnesota

Capstone Books are published by Capstone Press
151 Good Counsel Drive, P.O. Box 669, Mankato, Minnesota 56002
http://www.capstone-press.com

Library of Congress Cataloging-in-Publication Data
Green, Michael, 1952–
    U.S. Army Special Operations/by Michael Green
    p. cm.—(Serving your country)
    Includes bibliographical references and index.
    Summary: Presents the U.S. Army Special Operations Command, including the
various sub-groups, their history, missions, training, and equipment.
    ISBN 0-7368-0471-4
    1. United States Army Special Operations Command—Juvenile literature.
2. Special forces (Military Science)—United States—Juvenile literature. 3. United
States. Army—Commando troops—Juvenile literature. [1. United States Army Special
Operations Command. 2. Special forces (Military science)] I. Title. II. Series.
UA34.S64 G735 2000
356'.167'0973—dc21   99-053737

Editorial Credits
Matt Doeden, editor; Timothy Halldin, cover designer; Linda Clavel, production designer;
    Heidi Schoof, photo researcher

Photo Credits
Hans Halberstadt, 7, 10, 17, 32
Photri-Microstock, 18, 21
U.S. Army, 4, 8, 12, 14, 22, 25, 26, 29, 30–31, 35, 36, 40, 43
Walter Sokalski Jr., cover, 39

1 2 3 4 5 6 05 04 03 02 01 00

Table of Contents

Chapter 1
Special Operations

Members of the U.S. Army Special Operations Forces (SOF) are highly trained soldiers. Soldiers in the SOF perform specialized and dangerous missions. SOF members must be physically fit, skilled, and intelligent to complete these tasks.

The U.S. Army SOF includes different groups. Each group performs specialized missions. The three best known groups are the Rangers, the Special Forces, and the Night

Members of the U.S. Army Special Operations Forces are highly trained soldiers.

Stalkers. The Special Forces also are called the Green Berets.

Rangers

Rangers work together in large groups called battalions. Each battalion consists of about 600 Rangers. The Army has three Ranger battalions. Together, these battalions form the 75th Ranger Regiment.

Rangers are the SOF's infantry unit. These soldiers are trained in ground combat. Rangers are often the first U.S. soldiers to arrive at battle sites. Rangers sometimes travel to battle sites by airplane or helicopter. Rangers use strong, light pieces of cloth called parachutes to jump safely from airplanes and helicopters. Rangers gather information about enemy forces. This is called reconnaissance. This information helps other U.S. military forces prepare for battles.

Special Forces (Green Berets)

The Special Forces are trained in guerrilla warfare. Guerrilla warriors fight in small groups behind enemy lines. Special Forces

Rangers are the SOF's infantry unit.

Special Forces members must be able to survive for long periods of time in the wilderness.

members work in teams of 12. These small teams can move around in enemy territory without being spotted.

The Army often uses the Special Forces for quick surprise attacks. Special Forces soldiers are trained in hand-to-hand combat. They also must know how to use a variety of weapons. Special Forces soldiers must be able to survive for weeks or months in the wilderness. They must be able to move secretly through enemy territory without being spotted. This helps them plan attacks and perform reconnaissance.

160th SOAR(A)

The 160th Special Operations Aviation Regiment (Airborne) is a special support unit of the SOF. Members of the 160th SOAR(A) also are called Night Stalkers. This is because they often perform their missions at night. Night Stalkers provide helicopter support to other SOF units. Night Stalkers sometimes transport SOF troops or carry SOF supplies. Night Stalkers also perform direct action missions. On these missions, Night Stalkers use weapons aboard helicopters to destroy enemy weapons or bases.

Night Stalkers work in crews. Each crew includes a pilot, a co-pilot, and at least one crew chief. The pilot flies the helicopter with the co-pilot's help. The co-pilot takes over if the pilot is injured or tired. The crew chief has various duties. The crew chief controls the helicopter's weapons. The crew chief also loads and unloads passengers and supplies.

Chapter 2
History

The history of the U.S. Army SOF began during World War II (1939–1945). But the U.S. military has used specialized soldiers for more than 200 years. The American colonies formed Ranger units to fight Great Britain during the Revolutionary War (1775–1783). Rangers watched for British troops. Rangers reported any troops they saw. This gave American military leaders information and time to prepare for battle.

Rangers also fought in the Civil War (1861–1865). Both the United States and the Confederate States of America used Rangers

The U.S. military has used specialized soldiers for more than 200 years.

The U.S. Army's first modern SOF group was the Rangers.

during this war. The most famous group of Civil War Rangers was a Confederate group called Mosby's Rangers. Their leader was John Mosby. Mosby and his Rangers sneaked into land controlled by the United States. They blew up railroads and raided enemy camps.

Darby's Rangers
The first modern SOF groups formed during World War II. This war was fought between

the Allied forces and the Axis powers. The Allied forces included the United States, Canada, the United Kingdom, France, and the Soviet Union. The Axis powers included Germany, Japan, and Italy.

U.S. military leaders modeled the U.S. SOF after British commando soldiers. British commandos were highly trained soldiers who specialized in reconnaissance. Commandos worked in small groups to gather information about enemies. The first U.S. SOF group was the 1st U.S. Army Ranger Battalion. An Army member named William Darby led the battalion. People called the battalion Darby's Rangers.

Darby's Rangers performed many important missions during World War II. In March 1943, Darby's Rangers climbed a steep mountain in northern Africa at night. A large group of enemy soldiers was at the top of the mountain. The Rangers caught the enemy soldiers by surprise and captured them. In July 1943, Rangers captured a city called Porto Empedocle in Italy. The Rangers captured more than 700 enemy soldiers there.

During World War II, Rangers fought in island jungles on the Pacific Ocean.

Rangers also played an important part in D-Day. D-Day is one of the most famous battles in history. The German military had taken control of France during World War II. The Allied forces wanted to regain control of the country. On June 6, 1944, Rangers helped the Allied forces invade France. Rangers helped fight the German military during this battle.

The U.S. Army had six Ranger battalions by the end of World War II. Rangers fought in northern Africa, Europe, and on the Pacific Ocean.

Merrill's Marauders and Alamo Scouts

The Allied forces also fought the Japanese military on the Pacific Ocean during World War II. Much of this fighting was in island jungles. In October 1943, the U.S. Army formed the 5307th Composite Unit (Provisional). This 3,000-man Ranger unit was specially trained in jungle combat. General Frank D. Merrill was in charge of the unit. People nicknamed the unit Merrill's Marauders.

Merrill's Marauders' first major mission was to capture an airfield in Burma. The Allied forces wanted to control the airfield. It was the best place in the area for planes to take off and land. The soldiers had to march more than 1,000 miles (1,600 kilometers) through the jungle to reach the airfield. They also had to fight many Japanese troops along the way.

More than half of the Rangers died during this mission.

The Alamo Scouts were another famous World War II SOF group. Alamo Scouts worked in small teams of six or seven soldiers. They gathered information about the Japanese military. They also raided Japanese supply centers and bases. Alamo Scouts sometimes freed Allied soldiers being held as prisoners of war.

The Green Berets

In 1952, the Army created the first Special Forces unit. The Army used the Special Forces for guerrilla warfare during the end of the Korean War (1950–1953). North Korea and South Korea fought in this war. Each side wanted all of Korea to have a different kind of government.

The Army selected its best soldiers for the Special Forces. Many of the soldiers had been in World War II. They were experienced and skilled. Most had parachuting skills. Many spoke more than one language.

Members of the Special Forces wear green berets to set them apart from other soldiers.

In 1961, President John F. Kennedy visited the SOF's home base at Fort Bragg, North Carolina. Kennedy believed that the Special Forces would help keep peace in Vietnam. North Vietnam and South Vietnam were at war during this time. U.S. officials wanted South Vietnam to win this war. Kennedy thought the Special Forces could help. Kennedy also thought that Special Forces soldiers needed something to set them apart from other

17

soldiers. He gave them permission to wear green hats called berets. The Special Forces were soon nicknamed the Green Berets.

Recent History

Rangers and Special Forces have played important roles in many recent conflicts. Both groups fought in the Vietnam War (1954–1975). The success of the Special Forces in this war made them famous throughout the world. People wrote books and songs and made movies about the Special Forces in the Vietnam War.

In the 1970s, terrorists committed many crimes around the world. Terrorists hold people against their will. These people are called hostages. Terrorists demand money or favors in exchange for the hostages' safety. In 1981, the Army created Task Force 160 to fight terrorists. Members of this force were specially trained to rescue hostages and handle terrorists. Task Force 160 later became known as the 160th Special Operations Aviation Regiment (Airborne). Today, people call members of this regiment Night Stalkers.

Special Forces became famous throughout the world during the Vietnam War.

In 1983, SOF groups fought in Grenada. U.S. troops were sent to this Caribbean island to protect U.S. medical students. Rebels had overthrown Grenada's government. The SOF prevented the rebels from hurting the U.S. medical students there.

In 1989, the Army used its SOF to invade Panama. U.S. officials believed this country's leaders were helping drug dealers bring illegal drugs into the United States.

Night Stalkers and Rangers used parachutes and helicopters to take over an airport in Panama. A bridge separated the airport from Panama's military forces. Special Forces took control of the bridge while Night Stalkers and Rangers landed at the airport. The Special Forces prevented Panamanian troops from crossing the bridge to attack the U.S. soldiers. The U.S. military later captured Panama's leader. His name was General Manuel Noriega. U.S. leaders put Noriega in jail for breaking drug laws.

Special Operations Forces also served during the Gulf War (1991). In 1990, Iraq's

The SOF played an important role in the Gulf War.

military invaded the nearby country of Kuwait. The United States sent troops to protect Kuwait and other nearby countries. Special Forces units kept track of Iraqi troops. They also helped to train the armies of countries in the area. Night Stalkers rescued pilots whose aircraft had crashed. The SOF helped the U.S. military and its allies drive Iraqi troops out of Kuwait.

Chapter 3
Vehicles and Equipment

Members of the U.S. Army SOF use a variety of vehicles and equipment to perform their missions. They need helicopters for transportation. They use weapons to defend themselves from enemy troops. They also need survival gear to stay alive in the wilderness.

Helicopters
Special Operations Forces members usually travel in helicopters to their mission sites. The MH-47 Chinook is one of these

---

SOF members usually travel in helicopters.

helicopters. Chinooks can carry five crew members and as many as 65 passengers. They also carry powerful guns and missiles. Chinooks can travel about 194 miles (312 kilometers) per hour.

Another important SOF helicopter is the MH-60 Blackhawk. Blackhawks are smaller and faster than Chinooks. Blackhawks can carry four crew members and as many as 12 passengers. This helicopter's top speed is about 222 miles (357 kilometers) per hour.

The AH/MH-6 Little Bird is the lightest and smallest SOF helicopter. Little Birds can carry two crew members and as many as six passengers. The passengers ride on a platform outside the helicopter. Little Birds can travel about 174 miles (280 kilometers) per hour.

Weapons
Special Operations Forces soldiers' most common weapon is the M-16 rifle. This lightweight weapon is easy to carry. But it also is powerful. M-16 rifles have a range of about

The MH-47 Chinook can carry as many as 65 passengers.

1,800 feet (550 meters). A range is the distance a bullet can travel.

SOF members sometimes carry machine guns. These weapons are more powerful than rifles. But they also are heavier. Machine guns can fire many rounds rapidly. The Army's newest machine gun is the Squad Automatic Weapon (SAW). The SAW can fire as many as

750 rounds per minute. It has a range of about 3,300 feet (1,000 meters).

SOF soldiers use missiles to destroy large targets such as enemy aircraft. The Stinger is one of these missiles. Soldiers launch Stingers with missile launchers that rest on their shoulders. Stingers have a range of about five miles (eight kilometers).

The Army also trains SOF soldiers to operate enemy weapons. Soldiers must know how to use these weapons if they are ever in enemy territory. U.S. weapons may not be available in some places. SOF soldiers may not be able to replace broken or lost weapons with new U.S. weapons. They may have to use enemy weapons instead.

Other Equipment

SOF soldiers need a variety of survival equipment to stay alive in the wilderness. They must wear proper clothing for each mission. For example, SOF soldiers in jungles wear camouflage clothing. This specially colored

The M-16 rifle is a common SOF weapon.

clothing helps soldiers blend in with their surroundings. Enemies cannot spot them as easily.

Medical equipment also is important. SOF soldiers may spend days or weeks on the job. They must take care of their own medical needs. Important medical equipment includes bandages, medicines, and disinfectants. Disinfectants keep open wounds from becoming infected.

Soldiers carry other survival equipment. They may carry compasses to keep track of their location. They may carry radios to communicate with one another and with their bases. Some SOF soldiers carry night vision goggles. Soldiers wear these goggles to help them see at night. Soldiers can see as far as 450 feet (137 meters) with night vision goggles.

SOF soldiers use radios to communicate with one another.

Blades

Cockpit

Engine

Fuel Tank

Landing Gear

Tail Rotor

Tail

Tail Wheel

MH-60 Blackhawk

Chapter 4
Training

Members of the SOF are volunteers. They ask to serve in the SOF. These volunteers receive the Army's most difficult training. Many of the soldiers who begin the training cannot finish it.

Members of the Army who wish to join the SOF must be men between the ages of 17 and 35. Women in the U.S. military cannot be SOF members. Congressional law prohibits women from serving in jobs that could place them under direct fire from enemies. SOF members must have at least a high school education.

Soldiers who wish to join the SOF must be men between the ages of 17 and 35.

They also must earn high scores on intelligence and physical fitness tests.

Ranger Training

Rangers begin their training at Fort Benning, Georgia. Trainees must pass a series of tests. For example, trainees must be able to swim while wearing all of their clothes and carrying all of their gear. Trainees also must complete obstacle courses. These courses may include obstacles such as high fences, barbed wire, and muddy pits.

Trainees also practice other skills they will need as Rangers. They practice parachuting. They learn hand-to-hand combat. They also learn how to perform reconnaissance missions.

Trainees who pass their training at Fort Benning move on to survival training. Trainees receive mountain training at Camp Frank D. Merrill, Georgia. They learn to rappel from helicopters and down mountain cliffs. Soldiers slide down long ropes to rappel. Trainees learn to survive in swamps at Eglin Air Force Base in

Rangers learn to climb up and rappel down cliffs.

Florida. There, trainees learn to avoid venomous snakes. They also learn to treat snake bites.

Special Forces Training

Special Forces training takes place at Fort Bragg. Soldiers who volunteer for Special Forces training must first pass a pre-selection course. They receive both physical and mental training during this three-week course. For example, soldiers must run long distances while

Special Forces members learn to use many weapons.

wearing heavy clothing and carrying their equipment. The Army uses the pre-selection course to evaluate trainees' physical and mental skills. Army officials also look for trainees with leadership skills. The course helps the Army find soldiers most suited to becoming Green Berets.

Soldiers who are selected to continue training enter the Special Forces Qualification

Course. Soldiers call this course the "Q Course." Trainees learn how to use a variety of weapons in this course. They also go through language training. Trainees learn to speak foreign languages. All Green Berets must speak at least one foreign language. Some Green Berets can speak as many as four foreign languages. This helps them to survive in enemy territory. Trainees also learn specialties in the Q Course. Specialties include communications, weapons, and medical care.

Special Forces members receive additional training after the Q Course. Officers and enlisted members receive different training. Officers have higher ranks than enlisted members. Officers learn how to be effective leaders and how to give orders. Enlisted members learn how to work effectively in teams. They also learn how best to carry out officers' orders.

Night Stalker Training

Night Stalkers begin their SOF careers with Green Platoon training. Two schools are involved in Green Platoon training. One is for soldiers who wish to become Night Stalker crew members. These soldiers are usually high-ranking enlisted members. The second school is for Army pilots who wish to become Night Stalker pilots. All pilots are officers.

Soldiers' Green Platoon training lasts five weeks. Soldiers learn about the 160th SOAR(A). They learn how to read maps and how to use compasses. They learn survival skills and practice hand-to-hand combat. Soldiers in Green Platoon also learn how to use a variety of weapons.

Pilots spend 14 weeks in Green Platoon training. Pilots learn many of the same skills as soldiers during Green Platoon. But they also learn special flying skills. They learn how to use night vision goggles to fly at night. Pilots also must prove their ability to fly in harsh weather conditions. Pilots who complete Green Platoon are Basic Mission Qualified (BMQ). BMQ pilots can perform some Night Stalker missions.

Night Stalkers must complete Green Platoon training.

Night Stalker pilots may continue their training after Green Platoon. They must train for another 12 to 18 months to become Fully Mission Qualified (FMQ). FMQ pilots can perform the most difficult Night Stalker missions. Some Night Stalker pilots train three to four more years. This allows them to become flight leads. Flight leads plan Night Stalker missions.

Chapter 5
The Future

Some U.S. military officials believe the SOF will become more important in the future. These officials believe wars in the future will not be conventional. This means wars will not follow the patterns of past wars. Future wars may be fought with more technology. Large battles may become rare. The SOF specialize in unconventional warfare. This may make them even more important in the future.

Technology
Future SOF members may rely more on technology than today's members do. Computers

The SOF will continue to be an important part of the U.S. Army in the future.

may help SOF members plan and perform missions. Communications equipment is improving. This equipment may help SOF members stay in contact with one another during missions.

The SOF also may benefit from a new aircraft called the CV-22 Osprey. The Osprey is a tilt-rotor aircraft. It can take off and land like a helicopter. But it also can fly like an airplane. The Army will begin using the Osprey in the early 2000s. The Osprey's speed will help SOF members reach mission sites quickly and safely.

Missions

Some people believe the SOF will perform more humanitarian missions in the future. Humanitarian missions help civilians. These people are not in the military. During the early 1990s, SOF members performed a humanitarian mission in the African country of Somalia. Somalia was under the control of warlords at this time. Somalia's people were starving and sick because of the way the warlords ruled the country. The SOF protected

SOF members may play an increased role in training other militaries.

Somalia's civilians from these gangs. The SOF made sure Somalia's people had food and medicine.

SOF members also may play an increased role in training other militaries. They may teach allies of the United States how to form their own special operations teams. This will help these countries defend themselves against enemies.

Words to Know

battalion (buh-TAL-yun)—a large group or unit of soldiers in the armed forces

civilian (si-VIL-yuhn)—a person who is not in the military

commando (kuh-MAN-doh)—a soldier who is specially trained for reconnaissance missions

hostage (HOSS-tij)—a person who has been captured and kept as a prisoner

infantry (IN-fuhn-tree)—soldiers trained to fight on the ground

mission (MISH-uhn)—a military task

rappel (ruh-PEL)—to use a rope to move quickly down a mountain or from a helicopter

reconnaissance (ree-KAH-nuh-suhnss)—a mission to gather information about an enemy

regiment (REJ-uh-muhnt)—a military unit made up of two or more battalions

To Learn More

Bohrer, David. *America's Special Forces.* Osceola, Wis.: MBI Publishing, 1998.

Burgan, Michael. *U.S. Army Special Forces: Airborne Rangers.* Warfare and Weapons. Mankato, Minn.: Capstone Books, 2000.

Streissguth, Thomas. *The Green Berets.* Serving Your Country. Minneapolis: Capstone Books, 1996.

Weiser, Andrea. *U.S. Army Special Operations Command: Night Stalkers Special Operations Aviation.* Warfare and Weapons. Mankato, Minn.: Capstone Books, 2000.

Useful Addresses

JFK Special Warfare Museum
P.O. Box 70060
Fort Bragg, NC 28307

U.S. Army Public Affairs
1500 Army Pentagon
Washington, DC 20310-1500

U.S. Army Ranger Association
P.O. Box 52126
Fort Benning, GA 31995

U.S. Army Special Operations Command
Public Affairs Office
Fort Bragg, NC 28307

Internet Sites

Rangers Lead the Way!
http://www.ranger.org

U.S. Army
http://www.army.mil

U.S. Army Center of Military History
http://www.army.mil/cmh-pg

Index